HOW TO START A BUSINESS:
Step by step guides for establishing successful business

Michael E. Fox

in critical reviews and certain other noncommercial uses permitted by copyright law.

Table of contents

Chapter 1

Introduction
(being an entrepreneur)

Being an entrepreneur is not an easy profession, you need to have a certain set of talents to become a successful entrepreneur.

Entrepreneurs are risk takers, they are persons who generate fresh company concepts, carrying all the risks and reaping most of the benefits.

Entrepreneurs are also considered to be inventors. They come up with fantastic and beautiful ideas, implement them and they go through difficulties to make these ideas succeed.

To be categorized as an entrepreneur you will need to possess specific attributes that will be able to designate u as entrepreneur. Some of these traits include;

1.Creative

As an entrepreneur, you will need to discover unique techniques and ideas to be able to tackle most of the issues in your community and field of business. You are required to know the fundamental demands of your community and field of business and be able to discover solutions to fixing such challenges. For instance, if your town has an issue with a shortage of decent drinking water as an entrepreneur you are expected to build up a company selling bottled water. This would be advantageous for you in growing and thriving your company since you have been able to identify a proper market audience for your unique goods.

2.Knowledge of goods

As an entrepreneur, you also need to have a solid understanding of the goods and products you are marketing since you need to be able to persuade clients and target audiences why they need your products and the amazing qualities your items offer. It is also crucial to recognize that not all your clients will adore your stuff. Therefore you need to communicate with them, acquire their answer and feedback and utilize their ideas and feedback to create changes in your goods. So that you will be able to match the wants and desires of your consumers so that your bus will be highly profitable.

3.Networking

As an entrepreneur, you need to be open in the sense that you need to acquire the capacity to establish a connection with individuals, and business partners and make company acquisitions since you never know where your next opportunity lies. You also need to be able to accept new business ideas all these connections would help invest in your company and if they are pleased with it they will suggest it to others which will help you establish additional connections with people and assist increase your business.

Every entrepreneur wants more visits, more quality leads, and more income. Yet launching a company isn't one of those "if you build it, they will come" situations. So much of getting a business off the ground has to do with time, strategy, and the market, so examine whether the economic circumstances are favorable to start a firm and if you can effectively penetrate the market with your product.

To build and run a successful company, you'll also need to create and fine-tune a business plan, assess your finances, complete all the legal paperwork, pick your partners, research apps for startups growth, choose the best tools and systems to help you get your marketing and sales off the ground ... plus a whole lot more.

Having a fantastic company concept is just half of the

road. To be successful, you'll need to take a few measures to get it off the ground. To develop your company concept and put yourself up for success, try doing the following:

1. Create a business strategy.

Your business plan lays out the basics of your company, including how it's formed, what product or service you'll provide, and how you'll be selling it. Developing a business plan can help you uncover any roadblocks on the horizon before you get into operating a company.

2. Pick a company name.

Your company name is a vital component of your new business. It defines what you'll name on formal papers and on the company plan you'll share with investors. Since your name will originate from your company strategy and offers, it's better to develop it after you've created a plan.

3. Select an ownership arrangement.

Your business's legal structure might affect what you're accountable for and the taxes you pay. The most prevalent forms of business structures are sole proprietorship, partnership, limited liability company, and corporation. Throughout the process of beginning a company, you'll need to pick the most suited one for you.

4. Register your business.

Registering your company is the next step after picking an ownership structure. That way, you can verify you're functioning within the most basic legal limits.

5. Examine and comply with legal obligations.

In addition to adopting a legal structure and registering your company, there are additional steps to follow to guarantee your firm is running lawfully, including getting any business licenses and permissions. Licensing requirements differ by industry – for instance, if you're going to form a building business, you'll need the right construction licenses.

6. Apply for financing.

When you're establishing a small company, borrowing loans from family and friends may suffice. But, bigger businesses will demand more funding.

Startup capital is vital regardless of the sort of company you're starting. Whether you leverage loans, grants, or family and friends, having strong cash will help you to do more successfully and inexpensively establish your firm.

As illustrated by this list, establishing a company entails a whole lot of moving elements, some more thrilling than others. Brainstorming business names? Fun! Paying taxes? ... Not so enjoyable. The answer to effectively getting your company off the ground is to methodically organize and arrange your materials, prioritize appropriately, and remain on top of the status and performance of each one of these moving elements.

From registering with the government to getting the word out about your firm to making important financial choices, you'll need to take a broad variety of measures to establish a successful business.

What a successful company entails and what the advantages of launching a successful business

Chapter 2

Starting a business and benefits of starting a business

Starting a business requires analytical thinking, determined organization, and detailed record-keeping.It's important to be aware of your competition and either appropriate or improve upon their successful tactics.

You'll almost certainly end up working harder for yourself than you would for someone else, so prepare to make sacrifices in your personal life when establishing your business.

Providing good service to your customers is crucial to gaining their loyalty and retaining their business and make sure not only that the business is ready for launch, but you are as well.

To succeed in business today, you need to be flexible and have good planning and organizational skills. Many people start a business thinking that they'll turn on their computers or open their doors and start making money, only to find that making money in a business is much more difficult than they thought.

You can avoid this in your business ventures by taking your time and planning out all the necessary steps you need to achieve success. Whatever type of business you want to start, using the following nine tips can help you be successful in your venture.

Starting a business gives an entrepreneur freedom from the desires and whims of superiors. A person will not be worried by thoughts of whether he/she will be fired tomorrow or not. An entrepreneur will not be delayed wages, not pulled out of the weekend or vacation, and will not worsen working conditions. If a businessperson sees potential in IT, such as 3D technologies, virtual reality, or in new markets, such as trading in electronic cars, he/she can make a managerial decision to pursue these markets. The next positive side of the business is personal growth. Creating and starting a business is an opportunity to check what an individual is worth.

1. Get Organized

To achieve business success you need to be organized. It will help you complete tasks and stay on top of things to be done. A good way to be organized is to create a to-do list each day. As you complete each item, check it off your list. This will ensure that you're not forgetting anything and completing all the tasks that are essential to the survival of your business

2. Keep Detailed Records

All successful businesses keep detailed records. By doing so, you'll know where the business stands financially and what potential challenges you could be facing. Just knowing this gives you time to create strategies to overcome those challenges.

Most businesses are choosing to keep two sets of records: one physical and one in the cloud. By having records that are constantly uploaded and backed up, a business no longer has to worry about losing their data. The physical record exists as a backup but more often than not, it is used to ensure that the other information is correct.

3. Analyze Your Competition

Competition breeds the best results. To be successful, you can't be afraid to study and learn from your competitors. After all, they may be doing something right that you can implement in your business to make more money.

How you analyze competition will vary between sectors. If you're a restaurant owner, you may simply be able to dine at your competition's restaurants, ask other customers what they think, and gain information that way. However, you could be a company with much more limited access to your competitors, such as a chemicals company. In that case, you would work with a business professional and accountant to go over not just what the business presents to the world, but any financial information you may be able to get on the company as well.

4. Understand the Risks and Rewards

The key to being successful is taking calculated risks to help your business grow. A good question to ask is "What's the downside?" If you can answer this question, then you know what the worst-case scenario is. This knowledge will allow you to take the kinds of calculated risks that can generate tremendous rewards. Understanding risks and rewards includes being smart about the timing of starting your business. For example, did the severe economic dislocation of 2020 provide you with an opportunity (say, manufacturing and selling face masks) or an impediment (opening a new restaurant during a time of social distancing and limited seating allowed)?

5. Be Creative

Always be looking for ways to improve your business and make it stand out from the competition. Recognize that you don't know everything and be open to new ideas and different approaches to your business.

There are many outlets that may lead to additional revenues. Take Amazon for example. The company started out as a bookseller and grew into an eCommerce giant. Not a lot of people expected that one of the major ways that Amazon makes its money is through its Web Services division. The division did so well that when Jeff Bezos stepped down as CEO, the head of Amazon Web Services was named the new CEO.

6. Stay Focused

The old saying "Rome wasn't built in a day" applies here. Just because you open a business doesn't mean you're going to immediately start making money. It takes time to let people know who you are, so stay focused on achieving your short-term goals.

Many small business owners don't even see a profit for a few years while they use their revenues to recoup investment costs. This is called being "in the red." When you are profitable and make more than you need to spend to cover debts and payroll, this is called being "in the black."

That being said, if the business is not turning a profit after a substantial period of time, it's worth looking into if there are issues with the product or service, if the market still exists, and other possible issues that might slow or halt a business's growth.

7. Prepare to Make Sacrifices

The lead-up to starting a business is hard work, but after you open your doors, your work has just begun. In many cases, you have to put in more time than you would if you were working for someone else, which may mean spending less time with family and friends to be successful.

The adage that there are no weekends and no vacations for business owners might ring true for those who are committed to making their business work. There is nothing wrong with full-time employment, and some business owners underestimate the true cost of the sacrifices that are required to start and maintain a profitable business.

8. Provide Great Service

There are many successful businesses that forget that providing great customer service is important. If you provide better service for your customers, they'll be more inclined to come to you the next time they need something instead of going to your competition.

In today's hyper-competitive business environment, often the differentiating factor being successful and unsuccessful businesses is the level of service that the business provides. This is where the saying "undersell and overdeliver" comes in use, and savvy business owners would be wise to follow it.

9. Be Consistent

Consistency is a key component to making money in business. You have to keep doing what is necessary to be successful day in and day out. This will create long-term positive habits that will help you make money in the long run.

What Is the Fastest Way for a Company to Grow?

Companies will expand at their speeds, and many times this is beyond the control of the firm owner or personnel. Yet, certain features of operating lean may help a firm develop rapidly, such as concentrating on a narrow product line, scaling up instead of scaling down, and having some form of visible benefit over your competition.

How Do You Boost Sales?

Increased sales might come from a few different areas. You may enhance advertising expenditures where it has a proven impact, give recommendations from current customers, establish a direct-to-consumer email list, and others. You may also extend a product line, but if it underperforms, it will severely affect your bottom line.

Many hurdles come with owning your own company. For many individuals, nevertheless, the pleasures of owning a company far exceed the obstacles. 76% of individuals who opt to start their own small company are "somewhat satisfied" or "extremely happy" with their choice.

Operating a company may be interesting for many individuals and many different reasons. Whether you are searching for a flexible lifestyle, are keen to innovate, or just want more control over your job and earning possibilities, there are numerous advantages to starting your own company. These are just a handful of the largest.

1.Independence and Control

Have you ever worked a job in which you believed you could accomplish better if you had control over how the work was done? Let's face it, employment may be restrictive and sometimes doesn't enable you to leverage your knowledge and talent.

When you develop your own company, you do what you want, how you want, and when you want. You develop the product or service to the degree you believe is optimum. You have methods and habits that work best for you. And if you need a power nap in the late morning or afternoon to improve creativity and productivity, you can take one.

2.Financial rewards

Working for yourself implies that you're going to immediately enjoy the advantages of your company's great financial performance - unlike your former life as an employee when your firm earns large profits, you'll be personally rewarded. This is a wonderful driving aspect since it implies you're 100% dedicated to the success of the firm and can't simply sit back and coast.

3.A feeling of pride

There's nothing greater than developing your own successful company. Making your ambition a reality, and knowing that all your hard work has finally paid off is a terrific feeling and is worth the stress and long hours it took to get there. There are various methods by which you might acquire validation from professional groups; for example, you can be fortunate enough to earn grants or accolades for your hard work. Simply knowing you're in the tiny percentile of businesses that made it beyond the first

4.Freedom to Choose Your Decisions

As an entrepreneur and company owner, you have the final power to make choices concerning hours, schedule, location, interior design, menu, product selection, and consumers.

5.Maximum Flexibility

The primary reason most individuals desire to start their own company is the independence and flexibility entrepreneurship affords them, according to recent research. Benefits include scheduling flexibility to accommodate kids' schedules, university courses, or personal preferences.

Time is merely one of the flexibilities that you have as an entrepreneur. You decide your optimum working environment, and location, and whether you want to work outside, inside, at night, in the morning, on a computer, or with wood. It is all up to you.

Consequently, there are a lot of benefits to beginning a firm. The spectrum of advantages may also include psychological ease in conversation.

A company owner may pick his partners and speak with them freely. Nonetheless, an entrepreneur owns the entire management right to engage in contracts and agreements exclusively with those persons who are nice to him/her and whom he/she trusts. A businessperson does not need to tolerate inept and unproductive personnel since he/she may terminate them.

Chapter 3

Developing a business plan
A business plan is a document explaining a firm, its goods or services, how it makes (or will earn) money, its leadership

and employees, it is funding, its operations model, and many other aspects crucial to its success.

For every company to be successful, it must be launched and run with a clear grasp of its consumers, its internal strengths, its competitive environment, and a vision of how it will develop to compete in the future. A company also requires money to start, run, and develop. By taking the time to build a detailed business plan, you will have a potent weapon for obtaining investors. Your business plan is the path for your firm. It clearly describes where you are, how you got there, and how you aim to go.

Business plans are developed as a required vehicle for acquiring funds from possible investors, bankers, and other lenders. It is an important document when taking your firm public or selling all or part of a corporation. In fact, without one, requesting a bank for cash is meaningless. To lenders or possible investors, it not only gives information and discloses an opinion of your venture's viability, but also displays your management qualities. An analytical, objective business plan tells lenders that you are skilled, structured, and prepared. One that is inadequately researched, or makes unsubstantiated assertions implies that you are inexperienced and in their eyes...reckless. It implies your strategy has just a few minutes to create a solid impression and must stand alone as an initial sales tool. Perform the best work you can, and let it positively portray you as the capable, competent company owner that you are.

Creating a business strategy will take time, but it is well worth your effort in the long run. Not only will this document give vital information to outside investors and lenders, but it will also spell out the game plan from which to conduct your organization. This is, by far, the most critical application for your company strategy. It will become your blueprint and steer you toward accomplishing your entire company's objectives. A typical entrepreneur has a fantastic company concept but is seldom competent in all aspects of operating a firm. Excellent business plans are detailed, well-thought-out papers that offer the framework for entrepreneurs to make sensible business choices. Whatever the intended purpose of your business plan, make sure it's detailed, and accurate, and backs up all your assertions with data.

Most company plans comprise the following sections:

1. Executive Summary

The executive summary is likely one of the most crucial portions of the complete business plan. Fundamentally, it's the overview or introduction, crafted in a manner to attract readers' attention and take them through the remainder of the business plan.

Most executive summaries include:

Mission statement

Business history and leadership

Competitive advantage overview

Financial projections

Company goals

If you're planning to start or expand a small business, preparing a business plan is still very crucial. The plan should include all the major factors of your business.

2. Narrow down what makes you different.

Before you start whipping up a business plan, think carefully about what makes your business unique first. If you're planning to start a new athletic clothing business, for example, then you'll need to differentiate yourself from the numerous other athletic clothing brands out there.

What makes yours stand out from the others? Are you going to produce apparel for certain sports or athletic activities, like yoga or hiking, or tennis? Do you utilize environmentally friendly materials? Does a specific amount of your revenues go to charity? Does your brand encourage good body image?

Knowing your brand's placement in the market can assist you to build recognition and revenue.

Remember: You're not simply selling your product or service - you're selling a mix of goods, value, and brand experience. Go through these key questions and outline them before you get into the nitty-gritty of your business plan study.

3. Assess your market's circumstances.

One of the first things to ask yourself while you're testing your company concept is if it has a place in the market. The market will ultimately define how successful your firm will be. What's your target market, and why would they be interested in purchasing from you?

Go specific here. For example, if you're selling bedding, you can't simply include everyone who sleeps on a bed in your target market. You need to target a smaller set of clients initially, such as teens from middle-income households.

From there, you may answer questions like \show many teens from middle-income households are presently in your country?

What bedding do they generally need?

Is the market expanding or stagnant?

Incorporate both an analysis of research that others have done, as well as original research that you've gathered yourself — whether through consumer surveys, interviews, or other means.

4. Develop a marketing and sales plan.

Here is where you may set out your thorough marketing and sales plans that'll include how you intend to sell your goods. Before you embark on your marketing and sales strategy, you'll need to have your market study properly filled out, and identify your target buyer personas, i.e., your ideal clients. (Learn how to construct buyer personas here.)

On the marketing side, you'll want to address answers to queries like \sHow do you aim to reach the market?

How will you develop your business?

Which channels will you concentrate on for distribution?

How will you communicate with your customers?

On the sales side, you'll need to address responses to queries like \ What's your sales strategy?

What will your sales staff look like, and how do you intend to develop it over time?

How do you intend to scale for growth?

How many sales calls will you need to make a sale?

What's the average price per sale?

Speaking of average price per sale, you'll want to dig into your pricing strategy as well.

It might assist to already have a marketing strategy worked out to help you educate this component of your company plan.

5. Describe a financial strategy including company expenses, financing, and income estimates.

Describe your financial model in detail, including your start-up cost, financial predictions, and a fundraising request if you're proposing to investors.

Your start-up cost refers to the resources you'll need to get your firm started and an estimate of how much each of those resources will cost. Are you leasing an office space? Do you need a computer? A phone? Write out these things and how much they'll cost, and be honest and modest in your estimations. The last thing you want to do is run out of money.

After you've identified your expenses, you'll need to justify them by explaining your financial expectations. This is particularly critical if you're searching for finance for your firm. Make sure your financial model is 100% correct for the greatest possibility of persuading investors and finance sources to fund your firm.

Chapter 4

Financing the business and how to secure finance
What Is Financing?
Finance is the process of supplying cash for company activity, making purchases, or investing. Financial organizations, such as banks, are in the business of providing money to companies, customers, and investors to help them accomplish their objectives. The use of finance is crucial in every economic system since it permits enterprises to acquire things beyond their immediate grasp.

Put simply, financing is a technique to utilize the time value of money to put future predicted money flows to use for initiatives undertaken today. Financing also makes use of the fact that some persons in an economy will have a surplus of money that they desire to put to work to create returns, while others need money to undertake investment (also to earn returns), creating a market for the money.

There are two primary forms of financing accessible for companies: debt financing and equity financing. Debt is a loan that must be paid back frequently with interest, although it is often cheaper than obtaining capital because of tax-deductible concerns. Equity does not need to be paid back, but it relinquishes ownership holdings to the shareholder.

Starting up the company and locating an ideal location for your business

It requires money to establish a company. Financing your firm is one of the first and most essential financial considerations most business owners make. How you choose to finance your company might affect how you structure and operate your firm.

While there are different methods of getting finances for a company, some of the techniques for securing funds include the;

1. self-funding

self-funding enables you to harness your financial resources to assist your firm. Self-funding may come in the form of turning to family and friends for financing, utilizing your savings accounts, or even dipping into your 401(k) (k).

With self-funding, you maintain entire control over the firm, but you also take on all the risk yourself. Be cautious not to spend more than you can afford, and be particularly careful if you choose to draw into retirement assets early. You could incur significant costs or penalties, or ruin your chance to retire on time – so you should check with your plan's administrator and a personal financial counselor beforehand.

2. crowdfunding

Crowdfunding generates finances for a company from a huge number of individuals, termed crowd funders. Crowdfunders aren't technically investors, since they don't acquire a portion of ownership in the firm and don't anticipate a financial return on their money.

Instead, crowd funders expect to obtain a "gift" from your firm as appreciation for their donation. Frequently, that present is the product you hope to sell or other unique privileges, like seeing the company owner or receiving their name in the credits. This makes crowdsourcing a popular choice for those who wish to develop artistic works (like a documentary), or physical goods (like a high-tech cooler) (like a high-tech cooler).

Crowdfunding is also popular since it's incredibly little risk for company owners. Not only do you get to keep complete control of your firm, but if your plan fails, you're often under no obligation to reimburse your crowd funders. Every crowdfunding site is different, so be sure you read the tiny print and understand your complete financial and legal duties.

3. Venture capital

The first thing to bear in mind is that this financing source is not necessarily for all businesses. From the outset, you should be aware that venture investors are seeking technology-driven enterprises and companies with high-growth potential in industries such as information technology, communications, and biotechnology.

Venture capitalists acquire an ownership interest in the firm to assist it to carry out a promising but higher-risk idea. This includes handing up partial ownership or equity in your firm to an external entity. Venture investors also anticipate a strong return on their investment, generally produced when the firm begins selling shares to the public. Make careful to seek investors that provide relevant expertise and skills to your firm.

4. Loans

Loans are the most widely utilized method of capital for small and medium-sized enterprises. Consider the fact that every lender provides distinct benefits, whether it's individualized service or tailored repayment. It's a good idea to browse around and pick the lender that matches your demands.

In general, start-ups have a tougher difficulty acquiring financing than established enterprises. Entrepreneurs with sound business strategies and a decent credit rating are more likely to be able to acquire financing.

To boost your chances of receiving a loan, you should have a company strategy, expenditure sheet, and financial predictions for the next five years. These tools will offer you an indication of how much you'll need to ask for and will assist the bank to realize they're making a good decision by providing you with a loan.

After you have your papers ready, contact banks and credit unions to obtain a loan. You'll want to compare offers to receive the best available conditions for your loan.

5.Angels

Angels are often rich people or retired corporate leaders who invest directly in small enterprises operated by others. They are frequently leaders in their area who not only give their experience and network of connections but also their technical and/or managerial skills.

In exchange for risking their money, they retain the right to oversee the company's management procedures. In real terms, this generally means a seat on the board of directors and a pledge of openness.

Chapter 5

Marketing strategies

Building a company isn't simple. First, you need a credible concept. From there, you need to locate a successful niche, define a target audience and have something of value to offer them. Whether you're hawking items, services, or knowledge, getting the word out has become more difficult. Yet without the correct marketing strategy to drive your development, generating a profit and staying afloat is practically difficult.

Nevertheless, selecting the correct tactics to sell your organization is sometimes equated to rocket science. How can you deliver your message to the proper audience and do it effectively? How can you raise awareness and increase sales while preserving a profit with a converting offer? Nowadays, with so much fighting for our attention from social networking, to search engine optimization, blogging, and pay-per-click advertising, it's easy to understand why most are ready to rip their hair out.

As an entrepreneur, you need to know certain company marketing tactics that work, which are

1. Advertise your company online

When it comes to promoting your company, there are various tactics that you may utilize. Nevertheless, not all of these tactics will be helpful for your organization. To identify the finest digital marketing plan for your small company, you need to perform some research and test out a few various approaches.

One of the most popular internet marketing methods is social media advertising. This entails leveraging sites like Facebook, Twitter, and LinkedIn to market your company. You may develop advertising that targets certain demographics, or you can just post about your company on your social networking platforms.

As most people are on their mobile devices regularly, utilizing social media postings or Google AdWords to promote your company may be a better marketing option than employing direct mail initiatives. The internet also works as the heart of word-of-mouth marketing, with in-person experiences mirrored on review and recommendation sites like Yelp.

2. Know how to target your audience

A target audience is a defined set of individuals who are most likely to acquire your goods or service. It resides at the center of all your targeting and advertising tactics - as described in the figure below.

It contrasts with your target market – which is far larger and includes groups who 'may be interested' and persona targeting - ideal groupings of individuals who constitute ideal consumers.

When it comes to marketing your small company, it's crucial to target the correct audience. By designing a plan that focuses on your ideal customer, you'll be able to reach more individuals who are likely to be interested in what you have to offer.

The objectives you establish assist you to determine the target market to pursue. This needs you to become acquainted with the clients in this industry, which involves some degree of market research and analysis.

3. Set defined business objectives

Business objectives define what a firm aspires to accomplish over \ time. To be successful, corporate objectives should be clear and contain a timeframe by which they should be fulfilled. The clarity and the timing allow businesses to assess whether they've fulfilled their declared objectives — and, if not, to know by how much they've fallen short.

An organization may create as many objectives as it likes, and it can set goals for the company as a whole and for particular units inside the organization. Business objectives may also be separated into short-term goals, medium goals, and long-term goals. But all business objectives must establish a precise target the organization hopes to attain over the stated timescale, said Jennifer Jones, senior research adviser in the industry practice at Info-Tech Research Group and SoftwareReviews.

Your company's vision and goals are the driving reasons behind your marketing strategy. These general objectives assist set your marketing goals, which your marketing strategy is in service of.

Your marketing objectives build on your company's goals. You may establish a target to obtain a given market share, dominate a particular channel or reach a certain proportion of a certain sort of customer. Your objectives should be achievable and quantifiable.

4. Use influencers to create brand awareness

When it comes to promoting your small company, you can't

afford to underestimate the power of influencers. Influencers are persons with a significant internet following who can impact the thoughts of their followers. In other words, if an influencer endorses your product or service, their followers are likely to take note.

There are various methods to work with influencers to generate visibility for your small company. One approach is to reach out to them personally and urge them to join a marketing campaign to promote your product or service. Another alternative is to collaborate with an influencer marketing firm that can link you with influencers that are a good match for your business.

Ways in which influencers promote a company include

1. Content Creation

Handing over the content production keys to your influencer or influencers is fantastic for brand visibility. It is because your influencers understand your target audience (their followers) better than you do.

Influencers are better equipped to make an emotional appeal to an already engaged audience. Their following will likewise not be utilizing ad blockers; even if the influencer provides commercial material.

2. Run Contests with Influencers

Contests and giveaways are some of the greatest influencer marketing tactics to promote brands and generate positive buzz. Marketers may utilize them to expand their social media following and generate traffic to their websites.

A successful and unique contest approach will help influencers to establish an atmosphere that fosters interesting interactions. It would also encourage interest among the followers to sample the goods.

You should establish various contest techniques for each social media network that is acceptable for the audience on that platform. For example, Instagram and Facebook are excellent social media outlets to sell fashion and lifestyle businesses.

3.   Establish   Referral Programs for Influencers

The simplest and most successful referral program technique is to provide a discount code that is unique to each influencer. The influencers may then share the offer codes with their followers via their content. When the influencer distributes promotional links and discount coupons unique to their followers, it captures their attention and motivates them to visit the site or apply the code.

If you establish a referral program, always ask the influencers to promote the company name on their blog and social media platforms. When their followers see the influencer endorsing your brand, it develops social trust and boosts your brand recall value.

4. Ask Influencers to Contribute to Your Blog

When a highly well-known influencer from your sector submits a guest article to your site, ask them to promote the material. It's a terrific mutually-beneficial technique to attract traffic from numerous channels.

The influencer distributes the blog link, which generates both brand awareness and fosters trust among their followers. When visitors realize the influencer they trust has contributed an article to your blog, they see your site as more trustworthy.

With the correct social media influencer marketing plan, you can not only enhance your brand recognition but also transform it into a household name.

But for you to do this, you will need a perfect mix of three crucial components - the appropriate platform, the right influencer, and the correct approach. All three of them should complement each other.

There are various marketing tactics out there and a means to study and decide which one is ideal for your organization. Yet a more cost-effective method to evaluate which of these techniques perform effectively for your organization is to simply examine yourself and your firm as a whole.

Discover what your company needs right now.

You must also work out where you picture your firm in the following months and years. Contemplate it and anticipate the prospective development of your firm. Overall, always remember that you may execute several of these marketing methods at one time, but you may also do them one at a time and discover which works best for you. Following that, stick to what works, and don't forget to try new things.

Chapter 6

Conclusion

Register your business name

You generally won't need to take an extra step to register your company name. Most times, it will happen automatically.

If you are a new corporation or LLC, your company name will immediately be registered with your state when you register your firm, so you don't have to go through a separate procedure. There are restrictions for naming a company and LLC, which you may learn about here.

Whether you are a sole proprietorship, partnership, or existing corporation or LLC, register a "Doing Business As" (DBA) name if you wish to conduct business using a name different than your registered name. You may do so either by traveling to your county clerk's office or with your state government, depending on which state you're in. Discover how to accomplish it here.

If you're perplexed by the LLC, company, and partnership things, do not worry. They are called business structures, and they dictate how your organization functions from the top down. Following, we explore how to pick amongst them.

How to Select an Ownership Structure

Selecting an ownership structure, also known as your firm legal structure or business entity, is one of the essential legal criteria you'll need to meet when beginning your business.

The four most prevalent business structures are:

1. Single Proprietorship

A sole proprietorship is a company that's owned and controlled by one person, where the government recognizes no legal difference between the individual who owns the firm and the business itself. It's the easiest approach to handle the firm. You don't have to name your firm anything other than your own, personal name, but if you want to, you may give it its own unique identity by registering what's called a

Doing Business As (DBA) name.

Example

An independent graphic designer operating their firm without further aid or with legally outsourced labor.

2. Partnership

A partnership is a single firm where two or more persons share ownership, and each owner contributes to all parts of the business, including shares in the revenues and losses of the business.

Example

Many physicians operate different practices in the same facility.

In a company particularly when operating a big business you are required to recruit personnel so as ease the job in your business

Small company owners may recruit most of their family but major firm owners are required to operate with a huge labor force

Employing personnel provides unique prospects for boosting your company's income, capacity, and brand awareness. The perfect new hire may also

A new employee may offer abilities that take years to acquire, enabling you to seek new income sources, cover your company's skills shortages, and drive quick development with only one hiring.

Hiring a new employee provides you the option to offload chores and improve your bandwidth, enhancing productivity and freeing up time for you and your team members to concentrate on what's essential.

Suggestions on how to acquire competent and experienced personnel

1. Conduct your research

Prepare to recruit by looking at comparable job descriptions and examining resumes of suitable individuals to determine what skills and experience are necessary for jobs like yours. Track job trends in your location and sector to uncover the most popular job titles and keywords potential applicants are looking for and compare wages to decide the proper pay level for your function. To assist build the framework for drafting a competitive job ad, come up with a list of the major job functions your new employee will be accountable for and think about the attributes your ideal applicant will have.

2. Pick a highly-clickable job title

Publish a free job on Indeed using a clear, succinct job title that will rank high in search results and attract eligible people

1. Avoid keywords like "wizard," rockstar," or "ninja," as prospects are not likely to look for a job using such terms. Instead, choose a conventional job title that job searchers are looking for. For example, a detailed title like "Full Stack Software Developer" would show in more search results than "Software Guru" or "Full Stack Wizard."

Pro-tip: Job titles with 80 characters or fewer attract more clicks on Indeed.

3. Write a distinctive job description

To compete with larger organizations, implement best practices for clear, compelling job descriptions. Consider what your ideal prospect is likely to look for, then integrate these common keywords into your description for optimum exposure. Add accurate descriptions of the job's tasks, qualifications, and incentives to entice the proper applicants to apply, and maintain the tone of conversational, informed, and welcoming. Check out these job description samples to help you design your appealing job ad.

Pro-tip: Try advertising a Sponsored Position for improved exposure, and fast access to excellent applicants you may invite to apply.

4. Review candidate resumes

When you have multiple applications streaming in, it's

time to start cutting down your prospect pool based on their credentials. Filter out candidates who don't fulfill the primary job criteria by sending them a rejection email (Indeed includes a built-in rejection letter you can send with the click of a button!). To evaluate which resumes should be placed in your "yes" or "maybe" piles, search for the following signals that convey a narrative about the candidate's motives, experience, and work style:

Quantitative proof of a candidate's prior accomplishments

Longevity at former employment despite "job-hopping" may be widespread depending on the business

Clear career growth

Attention to detail (is the CV plagued with grammatical and spelling mistakes?)

Abilities and experience that are suited to the job description

After analyzing resumes, engage with your top applicants to learn more about their credentials. This can help you generate a short list of the top prospects and select who should continue ahead in the recruiting process. You may send emails to learn more about your candidates' experience or start arranging phone screenings and interviews.

5. Interview your top prospects

When interviewing prospects, start with a brief 15 to 30-minute phone screen to find out if they satisfy the basic job description and to discover if there is a mutual fit. Finally, invite at least three of your most promising individuals to an in-person interview. Ask strategic questions that expose their talents and credentials, significant personality attributes, and degree of passion for the task and firm.

The Equal Employment Opportunity Commission's best practices for employers describe how to minimize prejudice in the interview process by avoiding certain issues, such as age, color, marital status, etc. These are some general questions that are suitable to ask for any position:

Tell me about yourself.

Why are you interested in this position/company?

What are your strengths/weaknesses?

What professional accomplishment are you most proud of?

Describe your ideal work atmosphere.

For assistance adapting your questions to the position you're looking for, check our collection of interview question samples, along with job and industry-relevant questions you may ask to identify the appropriate candidate for your firm.

Pro-tip: Take notes immediately after each interview so you'll recall the qualities and flaws of each applicant more vividly when it's time to make your final hiring choice.

6. Verify references

Checking references is a terrific approach to acquiring more insights, checking abilities, and confirming that you're recruiting people who are being honest about their job experience and credentials. Obtain at least three references from your top applicants and give them a short call.

Consider asking your candidate's references three to five of the following questions:

Can you confirm the candidate's job title, duties, start and finish dates, etc.?

How long have you known/worked with the candidate?

Tell me about what it's like to work with the applicant.

Why did they quit the position?

What are their major strengths and weaknesses?

With all these tactics establishing a great company won't be an issue since you know how to come about your;

Creating a business strategy

Funding the company and how to get financing

Starting up the company and locating an ideal location for your business

Marketing strategies

Business registration

Employing workers

Understanding all this will enhance your company in no time.

www.ingramcontent.com/pod-product-compliance
Lightning Source LLC
Chambersburg PA
CBHW070750220526
45467CB00018B/1785